DRESSING A NATION
THE HISTORY OF U.S. FASHION

HOOPSKIRTS, UNION BLUES, *and* CONFEDERATE GRAYS

Civil War FASHIONS *from* 1861 *to* 1865

KATE HAVELIN

TWENTY-FIRST CENTURY BOOKS
MINNEAPOLIS

Dedication

Any Civil War book of mine deserves some thanks to my husband, Leo Timmons, who has been reading about this war for most of his life. Leo, I owe you for all your help with this book and everything you've done to make our life smooth and civil for so long.

This fashion book makes me think of my mother, Marie Havelin. Mom, you're still the most fun—and most energetic—person with whom I've shopped. Whether we were having tea sandwiches at B. Altman's or browsing through thrift shops and garage sales, you made the hunt for clothes an adventure.

Front cover image: Wide hoopskirts, shawls, and elaborate hats were all popular for women during the Civil War era.

Back cover image: This Union officer from Indiana fought for the North in the Civil War. Uniforms for the North and South (Confederacy) varied throughout the war, but generally Northern soldiers wore blue, and Southern soldiers wore gray.

Page 3 image: This American woman was photographed in hoopskirts and a traditional hairstyle in 1860.

Twenty-First Century Books
A division of Lerner Publishing Group, Inc.
241 First Avenue North
Minneapolis, MN 55401 U.S.A.

Website address: www.lernerbooks.com

Library of Congress Cataloging-in-Publication Data

Havelin, Kate, 1961-
    Hoopskirts, Union blues, and Confederate grays : Civil War fashions from 1861 to 1865 /
by Kate Havelin.
      p. cm. — (Dressing a nation: the history of U.S. fashion)
    Includes bibliographical references and index.
    ISBN 978–0–7613–5889–3 (lib. bdg. : alk. paper)
    1. Clothing and dress—United States—History—19th century 2. Fashion—United States—History—19th century—Juvenile literature. 3. United States—History—Civil War, 1861–1865—Juvenile literature. 4. United States—Social life and customs—19th century—Juvenile literature.
    I. Title.
    GT610.H38 2012
    355.1'40973—dc22   2010048808

Manufactured in the United States of America
1 – MG – 7/15/11

CONTENTS

Chapter One

WOMEN'S CLOTHES

For much of the 1800s, one woman defined the times. Queen Victoria ruled the British Empire from 1837 to her death in 1901. Victoria influenced life, including fashion, around the globe. *Old-fashioned, prim*, and *overstuffed* are some of the words people in the twenty-first century use to describe Victorian styles and attitudes. Clothing, furniture, and housewares were cluttered and heavy. Dresses were big and bulky.

Wealthy women often wore at least eight layers of clothes that could weigh as much as 30 pounds (14 kilograms). Here are the layers of a typical upper-class woman's outfit:

- **A SHIFT** (a plain linen or cotton dress worn under all other clothes)

- ruffled, knee-length linen underpants, called *drawers, or pantalets*

- **A CORSET** to shape a woman's bust, waist, and hips

- **A CRINOLINE** to expand a woman's skirts

- *two petticoats* worn under a woman's dress

- silk, cotton, or wool **STOCKINGS**

- **THE DRESS**

Britain's Queen Victoria, shown here in 1861, was a fashion icon in her time. Designers copied the styles she wore, and people worldwide wanted to dress like her. After her husband, Prince Albert, died in 1861, the queen only wore black in mourning.

LAYER BY LAYER

The support in corsets and crinolines was made of horsehair, whalebone, or steel. Corsets and crinolines were the nineteenth-century version of high heels—traditional, fashionable items that may look good but hurt women's bodies. A corset is a piece of fabric stiffened with stays. It laces tightly in back and restricts a woman's midsection. Corsets squeezed women's ribs, stomachs, livers, diaphragms, and gallbladders. Many women fainted or suffered dizziness, headaches, or stomachaches because of tight corsets.

Once a woman was laced into her corset, she stepped into her crinoline, a bell-shaped cage made of flexible hoops and fabric bands. Before crinoline cages were invented, women often wore a half dozen petticoats under their dresses to puff them out. Crinolines weighed less than layers of bulky underskirts and created wider skirts too. Some crinoline skirts flared 18 feet (5.5 meters) around.

Only three women in crinoline skirts could fit into an average-sized room. The New York Omnibus Company raised trolley fares for ladies with hoops from seven cents to twelve cents. Big hoops sprawled over trolley seats and aisles and blocked the doors.

Women often needed help lacing up their corsets. They had to be tied very tightly to emphasize the bust and hips.

FATAL FASHION

Some women died because of their fashionable clothes. The June 17, 1865, *New York Times* told the shocking story of Kate Degraw, "A Young Lady Dragged Two Miles [3.2 kilometers] by Runaway Horses." As Degraw stepped out of a horse-drawn carriage, her hoopskirt got tangled in the carriage steps. The horses panicked and ran off, dragging Degraw's head and shoulders on the ground. By the time the horses stopped, the young woman was dead.

Hoop-skirted women were nicknamed tilters because the lightweight hoops sometimes tilted, exposing women's ankles and calves. Showing any part of a woman's leg was considered shocking during the 1800s. That prompted women to wear pantalets. For the first time in American history, women wore pants. Pantalets were two separate pieces of clothing—one for each leg. The two legs tied at the waist but didn't cover a woman's crotch.

Once a woman was finally dressed, she wasn't done. Upper-class women were expected to change their outfits several times each day. They had simple day dresses for doing chores at home, afternoon dresses for visiting friends, and ball gowns for fancy parties.

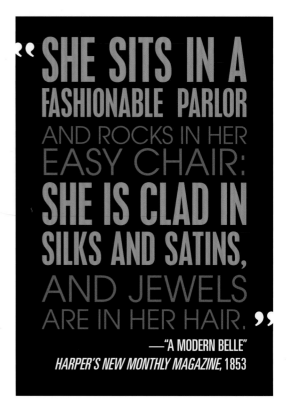

Women wore ball gowns such as this one to fancy parties in the 1860s. This photo shows Belle Boyd in 1862. From Virginia, Boyd was a spy for Confederate (Southern) troops during the Civil War (1861–1865).

"SHE SITS IN A FASHIONABLE PARLOR AND ROCKS IN HER EASY CHAIR: SHE IS CLAD IN SILKS AND SATINS, AND JEWELS ARE IN HER HAIR."
—"A MODERN BELLE"
HARPER'S NEW MONTHLY MAGAZINE, 1853

Girls' Clothes

Most young girls and boys in the mid-1800s dressed alike, in ankle-length pantalets topped by loose dresses or smocks that reached their knees. The loose clothing made it easier for kids to play. But it wasn't until the 1830s that girls began wearing pantalets. Some adults disapproved of girls wearing any kinds of pants, but the style made sense. Girls could jump rope without worrying about their skirts.

Many children had just two outfits, one for Sundays and other special occasions and the other for everyday wear. As girls grew older, their skirts grew longer and were covered by pinafores (white aprons that covered the front of dresses from shoulders to shins).

HOOPS OUT, BUSTLES IN

By 1864 a new fashion featured dresses with flatter fronts and full backs. Women tied bustles (padded rolls of wire, leather, or whalebone) around the back of their waists before putting on a dress. The bustles swept more of the dress fabric to a woman's back. It was difficult to walk or sit in a bustle.

WRAPPED IN STYLE

The children of Union (Northern) general Ulysess S. Grant pose in their best clothes for this portrait from 1862.

During the Civil War (1861–1865), American women loved wearing shawls, which kept them warm in drafty houses. One-size-fits-all shawls fit over even the widest of crinoline skirts.

Deluxe shawls were made from cashmere, superfine wool made from kashmir goats in Asia. It could take two men in India three years to weave one cashmere shawl. Cashmere is still one of the most delicate, durable, and costly wools.

Since most women couldn't afford premier cashmere, European weavers began making shawls of silk, ordinary wool, or cotton. The town of Paisley, Scotland, became known for making shawls with curvy teardrop designs. Paisley shawls were popular wedding presents and were worn by people of all ages in Europe and the United States. Even babies were wrapped in shawls. Shawls stayed in style until the bustle became the fashion. Bulky shawls didn't drape properly over bustles. People packed away their shawls, but paisley patterns remain popular.

Working Clothes

Women's clothes limited their ability to move freely and easily. Many women spent hours cooking, cleaning, and sewing as well as growing food, making candles, and spinning and weaving fabric. Some women worked as maids, cooks, laundresses, or mill girls in factories. Women who had to work for themselves or others needed practical clothes. They wore fewer layers. The clothes they wore included these:

- **a simple shift**
- **a corselet** (a front-lacing garment that was a shorter, simpler version of the corset)
- **a crinoline**
- **cotton stockings,** or hose
- **a dress** or simple skirt and jacket
- **an apron**

WOMEN WAR NURSES

During the Civil War, women stepped in to do jobs that had been traditionally men's work. Women ran farms and businesses. Women also became nurses, an occupation that had been held only by men until the 1850s.

Dorothea Dix organized American volunteer nurses during the Civil War. Dix demanded her nurses be plain looking, aged thirty or older, and able to cook. About three thousand women, including an aspiring writer named Louisa May Alcott, offered to nurse injured and sick soldiers during the war. Alcott's first book, *Hospital Sketches*, recounts some of her

WHO WEARS THE BLOOMING PANTS?

In the 1850s, a few brave women began wearing trousers, a fashion first. They wore loose-fitting trousers under knee-length tunics or skirts. Editor Amelia Bloomer *(below)* promoted the fashion in a newspaper she founded, called the *Lily*. Many other newspapers reported on Bloomer's shocking new fashion. Soon the trousers were called bloomers, after the best-known woman in pants.

The July 1851 *Harper's New Monthly Magazine* praised women who dared wear pants, for their "taste and courage," calling them as "bold as Joan of Arc [French heroine of the 1400s]." But most people mocked Bloomer and other dress reformers. Society expected women to wear long skirts.

By the 1860s, Bloomer had stopped wearing the trousers named for her. She thought they were taking attention away from more important women's issues, such as women's suffrage (the right to vote) and educational and employment rights for women.

wartime experiences. She gained more fame for a later novel, *Little Women*. Alcott and other Civil War nurses wore dark dresses without hoops. They weren't allowed to wear jewelry or curl their hair.

HATS and GLOVES

Almost all women wore some kind of head covering. Bare heads were not acceptable. Poorer women and slaves covered their heads with scarves, while middle-class and wealthy women wore hats.

Milliners—women who made and sold hats—molded felt, velvet, silk, and straw into countless shapes and kinds of hats. Ribbons, lace, beads, and feathers made hats fancier. Ostrich feathers were considered the top style because they were fluffy and could be dyed many colors.

In summer and winter, inside and out, a proper lady always wore gloves. The only time stylish women went without gloves was while they were eating. Short, kidskin gloves matched women's daytime outfits. Working women wore simpler gloves made of suede, wool, or cotton. For evening and formal occasions, women wore elbow-long, white gloves made of silk, satin, or lace. Nineteenth-century women also wore fingerless mittens that were knitted, crocheted, or embroidered to look airy and delicate.

Hats and gloves were must-have accessories during the Civil War era. Going out without a head covering of some kind was unacceptable for women.

This collection of accessories for women during the mid-1860s includes parasols, shoes, a brooch, and paisley shawls.

THE THINGS
SHE CARRIED

To protect their skin from the sun, women carried parasols. These decorative umbrellas were often made of silk and often with elaborate patterns. They also carried cloth handbags called reticules. Inside her bag, a woman could stash her

- **handkerchief**—made of plain cotton or fancy lace, a must-have for women and men since paper tissues hadn't yet been invented
- **fan**—made of paper, silk, feathers, ivory, or wood, a stylish way for heavily layered women to cool themselves
- **scent bottle**—tiny glass vials of perfume for masking odors from sooty chimneys, woodstoves, and sweaty, unwashed bodies
- **smelling salts**—made of ammonia and water for reviving women who felt faint from wearing tight corsets

FANCY BOOTS
AND **BARE FEET**

Queen Victoria set a new trend with balmorals—front-lacing everyday shoes that both men and women began wearing. For dressy occasions, women stepped into stylish pumps, which were low cut and had heels. At home, women wore mules (soft slip-on shoes).

Poorer working women depended on sturdy ankle boots and plain cotton stockings. But people who were extremely poor often went shoeless, even in winter. Many poorer people simply couldn't afford shoes. It was common to see poor children in New York walking outside barefoot year-round.

Face First

Queen Victoria and many doctors considered cosmetics improper, yet many women wore them. Women used soot from a candle to highlight their eyes or brows. Powder made from crushed flower petals gave women's cheeks and lips a hint of pink. Women also pinched their cheeks to add natural color. No woman wanted a tan. Pale skin was a sign that you were wealthy enough not to have to work outdoors.

ALL THAT GLITTERS

Jewelry gave women a great way to flaunt their style and wealth. A typical nineteenth-century jewelry box might hold

- **a brooch**—a decorated pin
- **a cameo**—a pin with a small stone or shell carved with the silhouette of a loved one
- **a posy holder**—a pin featuring a tiny cone to hold a flower bud
- **a watch**—attached to a pendant and worn as a necklace
- **a locket**—a small ornament that held a memento or a photograph, usually attached to a necklace
- **earrings**—small, delicate gold earrings for daytime wear, larger ones for evening events (one hole per ear)
- **a tiara**—a decorative hair ornament worn for fancy occasions
- **gold nuggets**—small bits of treasure from the 1849 California gold rush that adorned all kinds of items, from pins to necklaces
- **pearls**—especially popular for girls' jewelry

Women's daytime jewelry tended to be fairly modest. A typical woman might wear one or two pins, small earrings, and a watch pendant. By night, women glittered and sparkled with diamonds, rubies, and other gemstones. For evening occasions, women preferred matched sets of big earrings, pins, necklaces, bracelets, and a tiara.

HAIRY JEWELRY

Nineteenth-century Americans wore jewelry made from the hair of those they loved. Jewelers carefully twisted small locks of hair into pretty shapes and then glued the hair onto brooches or necklaces. Bracelets and key chains were made from braided hair.

When people died, some of their hair might be used to make mourning brooches and rings. Sometimes a snippet of hair was simply put inside a gold locket to be worn around a woman's neck or wrist.

Left: This locket from the Civil War features Varina Howell Davis, wife of Confederate president Jefferson Davis.

WOMEN'S HAIR

Throughout the 1800s, long hair—to the waist or below—was considered the only feminine hairstyle. But it wasn't proper for a grown woman to wear her hair loose and hanging down, except when she was sleeping.

During the day, women pulled their hair back off their faces. Most parted their hair in the middle and pulled it back neatly. Younger women might wear curls over their ears, but most wore their hair straight in front.

From the back, women's hair looked more ornate. It was gathered into a chignon, a bun of hair covered with a mesh or a net. Chignons usually sat at the nape of a woman's neck, where the head and neck meet. Some women added false hair, like modern hair extensions, to boost their chignons. Hair and chignons were often decorated with nets, spangles, jewels, pearls, ribbons, feathers, or flowers.

Braids and Curls

Poorer women swept their hair back in a simple bun, without fancy add-ons. Women in rural areas often pulled their long hair back in a simple braid.

Throughout the 1800s, girls wore their hair in simple braids or long, loose curls called barley-sugar curls. Girls and women wrapped their hair in pieces of cloth called rag rollers to create curls. Or they might use pin curls. Hair could also be ruffed (teased with a brush).

Americans in the 1800s didn't wash their hair often. But women brushed their hair a lot. Women often counted out one hundred strokes when brushing their hair at night. This frequent brushing spread natural oils that built up in the hair. It gave hair a fashionable luster.

A young woman reads a book, while a younger girl looks over her shoulder. The younger girl wears her hair in long curls, while the woman wears her hair pulled back in a bun.

A woman admires herself in a mirror in the mid-1800s. Her hair is arranged in a chignon with braids.

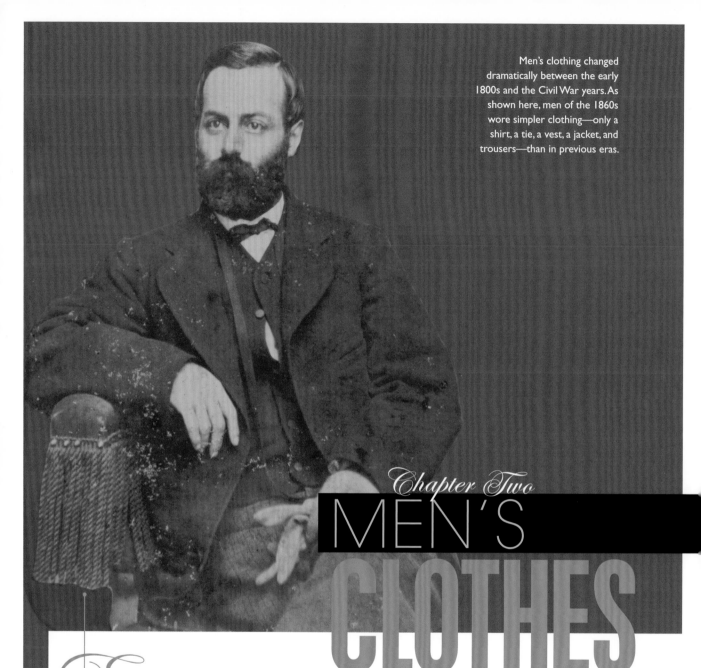

Men's clothing changed dramatically between the early 1800s and the Civil War years. As shown here, men of the 1860s wore simpler clothing—only a shirt, a tie, a vest, a jacket, and trousers—than in previous eras.

Chapter Two

MEN'S CLOTHES

Early in the 1800s, men wore lace ruffles, buckled shoes, and bold colors and patterns. As the century progressed, their fashions became simpler. Instead of ruffles, they wore plain shirts. Powdered wigs were replaced by short and simple hairstyles. Collars, ties, and coats were streamlined. By the Civil War, men's clothing styles were fairly plain and simple. Daytime clothes for most men consisted of six basic items:

- **A SHIRT**
- *a tie*
- **A VEST**
- **A COAT**
- *drawers*
- **TROUSERS**

BOILED AND BUTTONED UP

White shirts were a wardrobe essential for most men. But keeping those shirts white wasn't easy. Women washed shirts and other clothes by hand, soaking clothes in tubs of boiling water. That's why men's white tops came to be called boiled shirts. Laundresses starched and ironed the clean shirts crisp and stiff.

Some men wore fake shirtfronts called dickeys. These were man-sized bibs with collars that looked like men's shirtfronts. Since men wore vests and coats over their shirts, a dickey made it look as if the man was wearing a regular shirt. Dickeys were easier to clean.

The basic white shirt had long sleeves, but collars varied. Some were stiff and pointed straight up. Others folded over like wings. Whatever the style, collars got smudged fast

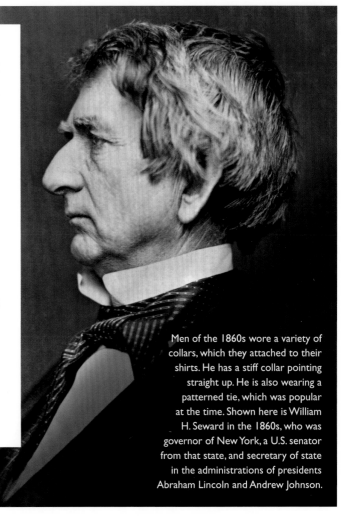

Men of the 1860s wore a variety of collars, which they attached to their shirts. He has a stiff collar pointing straight up. He is also wearing a patterned tie, which was popular at the time. Shown here is William H. Seward in the 1860s, who was governor of New York, a U.S. senator from that state, and secretary of state in the administrations of presidents Abraham Lincoln and Andrew Johnson.

This image shows a young man in the 1860s wearing a tie, a patterned vest, a jacket, and a turned-down collar.

from sweat, grease, and food stains. Some men wore detachable collars that could be washed separately.

In the 1860s, the latest news about shirts was the disposable collar. The collars were made of paper with a layer of linen glued on top. The disposable collars were printed with fake stitching.

Close to the Vest

Many men wore sleeveless vests with wide lapels over their shirts. While most other pieces of men's clothes were dark and somber, vests could be colorful. Men wore vests with flashy patterns such as plaids and checks. Men's vests were also called waistcoats.

Styles for men's ties seem to change often. In the 1860s, men looped ties or cravats (scarves) around their necks. Some men, such as President Abraham Lincoln, preferred narrow ties, which had been popular in the 1850s. Other men wrapped wide cravats around their necks and tied the ends in a bow. Men's neckwear was usually made of muslin or silk. Some cravats covered a fair amount of the shirt, leaving just some collar exposed.

Schuyler Colfax, a U.S. representative from Indiana in the mid-1860s and later vice president of the United States, wears a frock coat and trousers along with a shirt, a tie, and a vest.

COATS—
DON'T LEAVE HOME WITHOUT ONE

No matter what the weather, coats were part of men's daily clothes. Most men wore frock coats, which fit snugly around a man's chest and shoulders and then draped loosely to his knees. Most frock coats were black, but dark gray or blue were also acceptable. Dark colors were practical since soot from chimneys and factories tinged the air and settled everywhere.

When it was cold, men wore heavier coats or capes over their frock coats. A Chesterfield is a big overcoat with a velvet collar and several pockets. Inverness great coats feature big capes that drape over men's shoulders. Peacoats are short, heavy wool coats first worn by sailors but later popular with boys and men and, eventually, women.

MEN WEAR THE *Trousers*

Beneath all the layers was the most basic item of male clothing—drawers. The nineteenth-century version of underwear, drawers covered a man from waist to ankle. Drawers were made of cotton, flannel, or wool. They usually had two buttons in front and a fabric tie in back. Starting in 1863, knitting machines could mass-produce drawers, making a no-nonsense garment cheaper.

Stylish trousers were snug, not baggy. Some men wore pantaloons—trousers with a foot strap that looped under the shoes. The strap kept the trousers straight and close fitting. The pantaloon fad faded, but part of the name stayed—pants.

A STYLE THAT SUITS MEN— AND CRIMINALS

Some men liked the sack suit, a baggy square-cut coat with loose pants. But the nation's most famous detective, Allan Pinkerton, didn't care for the baggy sack look. In his memoir, *Thirty Years a Detective*, Pinkerton wrote, "As a rule, the men who steal the pocket-books and purses of ladies, wear a sack coat." Crooks could easily stash stolen goods in their roomy coats. Sack coats may have been thieves' coat of choice simply because they were less expensive. Sack coats were less fitted and could be bought ready to wear, which was cheaper than tailor-made fitted clothes.

Trousers often reached past men's ankles, making it tough to keep long pants clean and dry in muddy conditions. One day in 1850, an Englishman in New York was on his way to a wedding when it started to rain. The Englishman turned up his pant legs and showed up at the wedding with his impromptu cuffed pants. That sparked a style that's still around, rain or shine.

A TALE OF FORMAL CLOTHES

For parties and balls, upper-class men had just one option: white-tie formal wear. This meant a starched white shirt, white bow tie, white vest, and formal dress coat. The dress coats were new versions of old-fashioned frock coats that were cut waist-short in front for men riding horses. Evening coats were waist length in front and had two knee-length tails in back. Those long tails earned dress coats the nicknames tailcoats, swallowtails, or claw hammers. President Lincoln wore a black swallowtail coat at a formal reception in February 1862 to show off the newly redecorated White House.

Some tailcoats had an inside pocket for men's gloves, but the formal coats didn't have any outside pockets. And the buttons on a tailcoat were for decoration only. More than a century later, men still wear the same kind of white-tie formal wear. White tie and tails are a timeless classic.

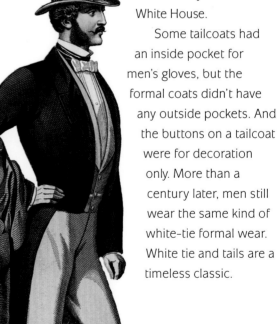

Formal occasions called for men to wear white-tie formal wear, such as shown in this drawing.

Play Clothes

Wealthy men could afford tailored clothes rich with fine details such as velvet collars and silk lapels. Although men didn't have as many different types of outfits as women, men with money could still dress well for any occasion.

One of the new trends was men's sportswear. Gymnasiums—special rooms for doing sports—started springing up in the 1800s. By the 1860s, men were competing in all kinds of sports, from gymnastics and golf to cricket and shooting. Back then, sporting men donned Norfolk jackets, which are boxy, hip-length tweed coats worn with belts. Instead of long trousers, men wore loose-fitting, knee-length pants called knickerbockers. Below the pants, men wore gaiters. These leather or cloth tubes buttoned around men's shoes and calves.

This man wears a Norfolk jacket and knicker-bockers for a shooting outing in 1860.

SAGGY PANTS WEREN'T IN STYLE

Men didn't wear belts to keep their pants up during the Civil War. To keep pants from sagging, men wore suspenders. Straps stretched over a man's shoulders, with the strap ends buttoned onto the waistband of his pants. Suspenders were a wardrobe basic for most men. It wasn't until the early 1900s that most trousers had belt loops.

WORKMEN'S WEAR

Poor and working-class men usually had just a simple wardrobe of sturdy wool pants and pullover shirts that buttoned halfway down the front. One common workman's garb is more beloved now than it was a century ago. Blue jeans were first made around 1853. In that year, New York merchant Levi Strauss went west to sell canvas tents to gold miners. But Strauss quickly found that miners needed pants more than tents, so he began sewing pants using

A JEAN BY ANY OTHER NAME

It's easy to see how Levi's blue jeans got their name. But do you know the stories behind the words *denim*, *dungaree*, and *jeans*?

- **Denim** comes from a French town called Nîmes, where a fabric called serge was woven. Levi Strauss first called his popular pants serge de Nîmes (serge from Nîmes)—but the name was soon shortened to denim.
- **Dungaree** refers to a kind of fabric from India. This denimlike cloth was called *dūgrī* in Hindi.
- **Jeans** got their name from material made in Genoa, Italy. The French people who wove that fabric called it Gênes.

Above: Levi Strauss of New York came up with the first blue jeans. Shown here in 1850, he is dressed in more formal clothing.

sturdy tent canvas. Soon he switched to a less stiff fabric that was dyed dark blue to hide stains.

Eventually, Strauss began reinforcing all the stitching, and he added copper rivets at the pockets. Miners and cowboys went wild for Strauss's well-constructed jeans. Those old pants are true collectors' items. In 2003 the oldest-known pair of Levi's in the United States sold for $46,500.

BLUE EYES MINE

Workers like these miners in California wore Levi jeans.

BOYS' CLOTHES

Very young boys and girls dressed alike, in white jackets with short-skirted tunics. By the age of six, boys switched to pants. Skeleton suits were common attire for boys. These snug-fitting suits included jackets that fastened to the pants with buttons all around the waist. The suits had seams that could be adjusted as a boy grew.

American boys also started wearing clothes made popular by Queen Victoria's children. The British royal family wore Highland (Scottish) clothing, including a knee-length, pleated skirt called a kilt, plaid stockings, and a matching sash. A small bonnet topped the ensemble. Another popular style that crossed the Atlantic was the sailor suit. This was a top with a big collar and shorts with white striped trim.

Sailor suits for young boys became popular in the 1860s. This child was photographed in 1867 in his sailor suit.

THE HATS *They Wore*

Hats were a big part of nineteenth-century men's style. Like women, men were expected to keep their heads covered in public. Two of the century's most recognized men—the U.S. president and Britain's prince—were known for their hats. The tall black hats President Lincoln wore were called top hats, stovepipe hats, chimney pots, and opera hats. Some top hats rose 8 inches (20 centimeters) above a man's head. Prince Albert, husband of Britain's Queen Victoria, popularized a hat called a boater. Boaters were wide-brimmed, low-crowned straw hats.

In the 1860s, a Philadelphia hatmaker went west and made a name for himself. John Batterson Stetson created the standard cowboy hat, available in just two colors—black or white. First sold in 1865, Stetson

Above: The Stetson was first sold to cowboys in the late 1800s. This was the Boss of the Plains model.

hats are made of fine felt with wide brims. Supposedly, Stetson hats had crowns deep enough for cowboys to use as buckets in an emergency. The hats originally cost twenty dollars—a huge amount of money, considering a cowboy earned thirty dollars a month. But once a cowboy had his Stetson, it lasted a lifetime.

A few other fashionable hats of the 1860s also sport the names of people or places:

- **gibus**—named for inventor Antoine Gibus, an opera hat with small springs inside so the hat could flatten to fit under a theater seat
- **derby**—named for the English Earl of Derby; formal, rounded hats made of soft felt with moderate brims and crowns creased in front and back; called bowlers by the British
- **Panama**— light-colored, lightweight straw hats made in Ecuador and named for the Isthmus of Panama from where they were shipped

Men also wore hats inside, a practical style for often chilly houses. They donned colorful, embroidered smoking caps for relaxing at home. For bedtime, they slipped on simple nightcaps.

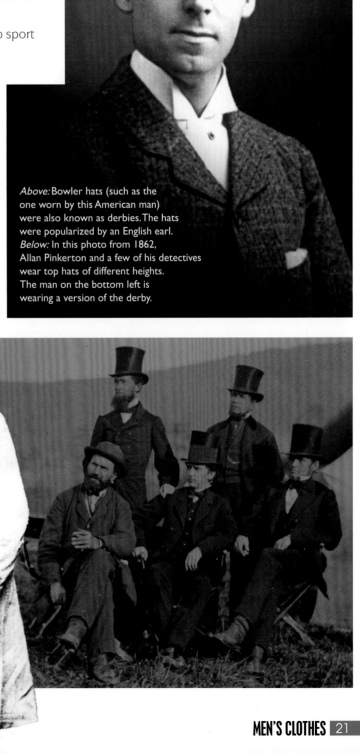

Above: Bowler hats (such as the one worn by this American man) were also known as derbies. The hats were popularized by an English earl. *Below:* In this photo from 1862, Allan Pinkerton and a few of his detectives wear top hats of different heights. The man on the bottom left is wearing a version of the derby.

Right: Famous Civil War photographer Mathew Brady wears a Panama hat in this photo from 1861.

Watching the Gold

Even before the 1849 gold rush, nineteenth-century men liked to flash their gold. They wore gold rings, pins, cuff links, and chains. Men wore tiepins studded with jewels to hold their neckwear in place and cuff links to keep their shirtsleeves from flapping open. Cuff links sparkled with gold, diamonds, silver, or ivory.

Many men carried pocket watches with small chains that fastened to their vests. The watches fit into tiny vest pockets and could be pulled out whenever a man wanted to check the time. Watch chains often had fobs, or small ornaments—another way for men to add some bling to their sober suits. Some men had fobs braided with hair from someone special.

Above: Many men carried pocket watches in the 1860s, with chains fastening them to their vests.

A GUY'S LITTLE NECESSITIES

Men of the 1860s kept a few everyday basics in their pockets. Manly must-have items included these:

- **gloves**—for horseback riding, traveling, and evening wear (President Lincoln wore white kid gloves for formal White House parties. He said his big, calloused hands looked like hams wrapped in canvas.)
- **handkerchief**—to wipe their noses and faces (Women would sprinkle perfume on a hanky and then give it to a beloved for remembrance.)
- **tobacco**—pipes, chewing tobacco, and cigars were popular. The first manufactured cigarettes, Bull Durhams, were made in 1860 but weren't widely popular until the 1900s.
- **weapon**—the derringer was the weapon of choice for many civilians. (Gamblers and dance hall women liked the compact, one-shot, derringer pistol, nicknamed the parlor gun. Some men preferred to carry a knife for protection.)

BOOTING UP *and* BIG FEET

Boots, the most common footwear for nineteenth-century men, were stylish and practical. Streets were unpaved and often muddy or littered with horse manure. Boots or high-cut shoes kept men's feet and trousers clean. Common nineteenth-century boot and shoe styles included these:

- **brogans**—heavy ankle-high shoes for workers and soldiers
- **Hessians**—boots that reached the knee and were perfect for horseback riding
- **Alberts**—shoes that laced on the side and had cloth tops with fancy buttons. Alberts were named for Britain's Prince Albert.

FAMOUS FOOTWEAR

Abraham Lincoln's feet were often sore. It was hard for him to find shoes that fit his big, size 14 feet. When he was newly married, Lincoln wore black velvet slippers that his wife, Mary, had embroidered with his initials. He sometimes even wore slippers when meeting White House guests, which shocked people who were used to more formal attire.

A few months before he died in 1865, Lincoln finally found boots that fit. He heard about a New York shoemaker named Dr. Zacharie who slipped felt between layers of leather to prevent blisters. Lincoln sent the shoemaker a piece of paper with the traced outline of his long, thin feet. The president enjoyed Zacharie's custom-made boots *(left)* so much he wrote a testimonial that the shoemaker used in advertisements.

To protect their pants, some men also wore gaiters, or spats (short for splatterdashes). The cloth leg coverings buttoned up on the side and shielded a man's shoes and pants from dust and mud. Gaiters didn't help keep feet warm, though, so some men stuffed straw or newspaper into their boots and shoes.

For parties, men wore pumps or other thin-soled shoes that were better for dancing. At home, men often wore slippers.

Two men discuss Civil War strategy in this photo from 1863. They are wearing Hessian boots and are smoking pipes. During the Civil War, the federal (Union) government began to tax tobacco to help pay for the war.

A Manly STYLE

For most of the 1700s and early 1800s, men were clean shaven. Then, in the 1850s, men in Europe began sporting beards and mustaches. The style started with British soldiers stationed in India. Indians considered facial hair manly, so British soldiers serving there grew mustaches. By 1854 mustaches were mandatory for soldiers in the East India Company in Bombay (present-day Mumbai).

Soon, men in Europe and the United States were experimenting with all kinds of facial hair. Northern Civil War generals Ulysses S. Grant, William T. Sherman, John Rawlings, and Frederick Dent displayed beards. So did Confederate generals Robert E. Lee, Thomas "Stonewall" Jackson, J. E. B. Stuart, and Nathan Bedford Forrest.

THE NAME OF THE HAIR

Union general Ambrose Burnside *(right)* became known for dramatic facial hair. His chin was clean shaven, but Burnside's cheeks were covered with whiskers that connected the hair on his head to his mustache. People called these side whiskers "burnsides." These days, we call them sideburns. Big, bushy sideburns that reach to the edge of a man's mouth are also known as mutton chops, since they're shaped a bit like the cut of meat by this name.

Union general Ulysses S. Grant *(right)* and Confederate general Robert E. Lee *(far right)* both wore full beards during the Civil War.

PRESIDENT LINCOLN'S FASHION FIRST

Abraham Lincoln did something that no president before him had done. Lincoln went to the White House with a beard. The fifteen presidents before Lincoln were all clean shaven. Lincoln's beard inaugurated a new look for presidents. Nine of the next eleven presidents after Lincoln had beards or mustaches. Only Andrew Johnson and William McKinley were clean shaven.

Presidential candidate Abraham Lincoln was clean shaven in October 1860 when he received this letter from a New Yorker named Grace Bedell: "I am a little girl only 11 years old, but want you should be President of the United States very much."

Grace wrote Lincoln that "if you let your whiskers grow . . . you would look a great deal better for your face is so thin." Lincoln answered Grace, but he didn't promise to stop shaving. But a month later, Lincoln had a trim beard. On the way to Washington, D.C., Lincoln's train stopped in Westfield, New York, Grace's hometown. He told townspeople about Grace's letter. Young Grace got to meet the new president, who leaned down and gave her a kiss, giving her a close-up brush with his famous whiskers. These days, Westfield, New York, features a statue of the little girl who inspired Lincoln to grow a beard.

Lincoln was clean shaven *(top)* when he was first a presidential candidate in 1860. Later, he grew a beard, which some attributed to the influence of a little girl from New York who wrote to Lincoln in 1860.

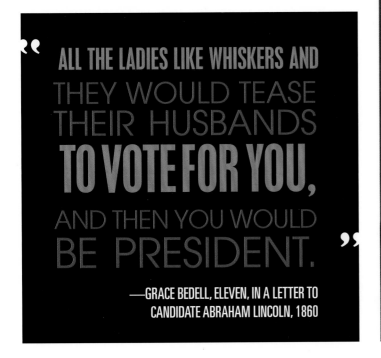

" ALL THE LADIES LIKE WHISKERS AND THEY WOULD TEASE THEIR HUSBANDS TO VOTE FOR YOU, AND THEN YOU WOULD BE PRESIDENT. "

—GRACE BEDELL, ELEVEN, IN A LETTER TO CANDIDATE ABRAHAM LINCOLN, 1860

Slaves in the United States generally only had one or two pairs of clothing for the entire year. This photo was taken in Savannah, Georgia, in the mid-1800s.

Chapter Three

SLAVES' CLOTHES

In 1860 four million African Americans were slaves in the United States. Slaves made up 13 percent of the U.S. population. Slaves received two sets of clothes a year from their owners—one for winter and one for summer. Frederick Douglass, a former slave who became one of the country's greatest public speakers, detailed the meager outfits of male slaves:

Their yearly clothing consisted of two coarse linen shirts, one pair of linen trousers . . . one jacket, one pair of trousers for winter, made of coarse . . . cloth, one pair of stockings, and one pair of shoes; the whole of which could not have cost more than seven dollars.

One slave owner's records showed he did spend just seven dollars on each slave's clothes, plus another dollar for shoes. That same owner spent three hundred dollars for one slave.

Female slaves' wardrobes were also scant. Each year a woman slave received these:

- ## TWO COARSE LINEN KNEE LENGTH SHIFTS

- ## *one jacket*

- ## ONE LINEN PETTICOAT SKIRT
  for summer

- ## ONE WOOL PETTICOAT SKIRT
  for winter

Most slave children didn't get even one full set of clothes. Young children and teens as old as fifteen often wore a single piece of clothing—a long shirt. In his autobiography, Douglass recalled his childhood as a slave, wearing just a dirty shirt and sleeping on a cold floor without even a blanket. He wrote in his autobiography: "I suffered much from hunger, but much more from cold. In hottest summer and coldest winter, I was kept almost naked—no shoes, no stockings, no jacket, no trousers, nothing on but a coarse [scratchy] linen shirt, reaching only to my knees."

These two African American boys were photographed in the 1860s. Slave children often had fewer clothes than adult slaves.

HARD SHOES,
SCRATCHY SHIRTS

Plantation owners gave slaves coarse fabric and cheap leather for their clothes and shoes. Slave women made their clothing. Slave men made the shoes. One former slave said his shoes were so hard they had to soften near the fire and be rubbed with grease before they could be worn.

One of the top inventors in the United States, Booker T. Washington, wrote that his "most trying ordeal" as a slave was wearing

Right: A bundle of flax shows the coarseness of the fibers.
Below: African Americans pick cotton in Georgia in this photo in the mid-1800s. Slaves often had to endure hot or cold conditions without proper clothes to protect their skin.

> ## "ALL OF OUR CLOTHING WAS HOMESPUN, OUR SOCKS WERE KNITTED... WE HAD OUR LOOMS AND MADE OUR OWN SUITS."
> —CLAYTON HOLBERT, FORMER SLAVE, 1937[1]

a new shirt made of flax. Flax is a plant used to make linen, but slaves didn't get soft linen. Instead, their clothes were made of coarse and scratchy flax. Washington wrote, "I can scarcely imagine any torture except, perhaps, the pulling of a tooth, that is equal to that caused by putting on a new flax shirt for the first time." In his autobiography, Washington remembered how grateful he was that his older brother John offered to wear his new flax shirt until it was less prickly.

Whether the clothes were made of flax or other coarse fabric, one or two outfits weren't enough to keep most slaves properly dressed for a year. Slaves' clothes wore out fast, damaged by sweat and grime, faded by the brutal southern sun, and torn by tough working conditions. Slaves often ended up wearing tattered shreds of clothes. Some were forced to go naked. They had to work in the fields without any clothing to protect them from the sun or cold.

SUNDAY BEST

Many slaves managed to buy a few extra pieces of clothing. They earned money by performing music or selling their homegrown vegetables or chickens. Some slaves did extra chores at night on their plantations to earn money. They used their hard-earned cash to buy special clothes. Slaves could wear their own clothes on Sundays, when most slaves had the day off and went to church. Slaves wore their Sunday best for holidays, funerals, and other special occasions.

They found creative ways to make clothes pretty and stylish. Some young slave women looped grapevines into makeshift crinoline hoops to fluff out their skirts. Slaves' Sunday clothes were often brightly colored. Former slave Tempe Herndon Durham remembered the dye-making skill of a slave woman who "knew every kind of root, bark, leaf an' berry dat made red, blue, green, or whatever color she wanted." Slaves wove their colorful cloth into rainbows of patterns. The striking combinations of stripes and checks were similar to African clothing styles.

This photo of slaves on a plantation in South Carolina shows a multigenerational family in their Sunday best.

KEEPING AFRICAN TRADITIONS

The amazing colors and patterns of slaves' Sunday clothing were one way that slaves kept their African heritage alive. Despite the many limits constricting their lives, slaves held on to their cultural history in ways big and small. For example, they:

- made charm bags (small pieces of fabric wrapped around items such as rabbits' feet, snakeskin, or horsehair, to bring luck)
- wrapped kerchiefs around their heads in the same styles as people did in Africa
- wore earrings, as their ancestors in Africa did. (Both male and female slaves wore earrings.)

Some slaves took care of their owners' children, such as this woman photographed in the 1850s. The woman is wearing a patterned shirt, as well as earrings, as many slaves did.

THE POWER OF CLOTHES

Enslaved people wanted to look good. They carried their neatly shined Sunday boots to church rather than wear them on the dusty or muddy roads. They traded clothes. They sometimes borrowed clothes from their owners for special occasions such as weddings.

Some slave owners didn't like seeing slaves dressed in their bright Sunday best. Some states passed laws banning slaves from dressing in fancy clothes. But many white owners gave their slaves extra clothes as a way to reward them or to motivate them to do more work.

Slaves who worked in plantation owners' homes had nicer clothing. While field slaves wore dusty rags that barely covered them, house slaves had modest shirts, trousers, and dresses. Slave drivers—slaves who were picked by their owners to be in charge of other slaves—wore the best clothes of all, including a decent coat and boots. Slave drivers also had whips. Instead of whipping slaves themselves, plantation owners had their slave drivers punish fellow slaves.

House slaves, such as these in Florida, ususally dressed in finer clothes than the slaves who worked in the fields.

THE CLOTHESLINE SPIES

During the Civil War, one husband-wife team of former slaves in Virginia found an ingenious way to use clothes to help the Union army. In 1863 Mrs. Dabney worked as a laundress for Confederate officers in Virginia. Across the Rappahannock River, her husband cooked for Union troops.

As she worked, Mrs. Dabney would often overhear information about the positions of Southern soldiers. The Dabneys came up with a clever code system to pass information about where Confederate troops were. For example, Mrs. Dabney could use a white shirt to represent Confederate general Stonewall Jackson and a gray jacket for Confederate general James Longstreet. When General Jackson moved his troops to the east, Mrs. Dabney hung a white shirt on the east end of her clothesline. When General Longstreet marched west, Mrs. Dabney moved a gray jacket to the west end of her line.

Across the river on the Union side, Mr. Dabney watched the changing laundry news and told Union officers about the enemy's troop movements. The secret clothesline communications helped the North.

This is an illustration of the 1862 Second Battle of Bull Run (or, Second Manassas as it was known in the South) in Virginia. It shows Union soldiers in blue and Confederate soldiers in gray. The illustration was published by Currier and Ives in the early 1860s.

Chapter Four

SOLDIERS' CLOTHES

When the Civil War began in 1861, both the North and the South had to gather and equip their armies. Soldiers needed uniforms, weapons, and other gear. The Union army of the North, also known as the Federals, wore dark blue. The Confederate army of the South, sometimes called the Rebels, chose gray.

In the beginning, both sides were short of standard uniforms. Soldiers sometimes wore civilian (nonmilitary) clothes. Some groups of soldiers assembled their own uniforms. At the 1861 Battle of Bull Run, makeshift uniforms cost lives. Some Northern troops wore gray, the official color of the Confederate army. Some Confederates wore blue, the color of the Union. Union gunners saw soldiers in blue approaching and thought they were Union troops coming to help. Instead, the blue soldiers were Confederates who ended up winning the battle. That battle proved it could be fatal to dress in the enemy's colors. Both armies began issuing more standard uniforms.

THE LANGUAGE OF UNIFORMS

Opposing armies usually wear different colors so they can easily identify friend from foe. But even within one army, uniforms tell a lot about a soldier.

Officers, the leaders in charge of groups of soldiers, usually wear specialized uniforms and insignia to show their roles. Insignia are designs such as stars *(shown in top photo of Union general William T. Sherman)* or crossed swords on the shoulders indicating an officer's rank. Lower-ranking noncommissioned officers wear chevrons, V-shaped stripes on the sleeves *(shown in the bottom photo of a Confederate army corporal)*.

Most Civil War soldiers were in the infantry. They were foot soldiers who needed basic uniforms with shoes rugged enough for long marches. Cavalry soldiers rode horses, so they wore shorter jackets, boots, and pants reinforced at the seat and legs. Artillery troops fire cannons. Union sharpshooters (expert marksmen) wore green uniforms—probably so they could blend in better with trees for camouflage.

Enlisted Union troops wore coat buttons stamped with an eagle, a symbol of the United States. Union officers and all Confederate officers and soldiers wore buttons stamped with an *I*, a *C*, or an *A* for infantry, cavalry, or artillery.

All soldiers' caps had a brass number and letter on the front showing their regiment and company (a smaller group within an army). Both armies used a color on the top of caps to show soldiers' jobs. Yellow was for cavalry, red was for artillery, and blue was for infantry.

UNION BLUES

The average Northern soldier received

- **ONE PAIR OF DRAWERS** (which many soldiers chose not to wear)
- *one pair of wool socks*
- **ONE PAIR OF FLANNEL, SKY-BLUE TROUSERS** with tin buttons
- **ONE COARSE BLUE WOOL SHIRT**
- **ONE DARK BLUE SACK COAT** with four brass buttons
- *one blue cap*
- **ONE PAIR OF SHOES**

This Union soldier has a plaid shirt underneath his uniform. Many soldiers had to make do with whatever they could come up with for clothing while serving in the military.

Above: This Union soldier is outfitted in a uniform that includes a kepi hat, trousers, a coat, and shoes. He is carrying a bayonet. Although many soldiers carried bayonets, bayonets were seldom used in Civil War battles.

Union soldiers also wore kepis (squashed-looking hats with visors). Kepis were also known as forage caps since soldiers used them to carry berries or nuts while foraging (searching for food).

When the war first started, Union soldiers were issued boots, which weren't comfortable for walking long distances. Most foot soldiers preferred to wear sturdy, ankle-high brogans.

The army-issue blue shirt each Union soldier received seldom lasted a full year. Many soldiers wore homespun shirts made by their families. Homemade shirts were often either white linen or plaid flannel. Many soldiers also added vests, which weren't part of the official uniform. The Union army had a dress code—specific rules for what soldiers should wear and how they should wear it. Soldiers could be fined if they didn't have at least the top button of their sack coat buttoned. As the war dragged on, dress codes were enforced less. But most Union troops wore at least most parts of their standard uniforms.

BLACK *and* BLUE

Some soldiers were particularly proud to wear the uniforms of the Union army. From the early days of the war, many African Americans, both free and enslaved, wanted to fight for the Union. At first, President Lincoln and his generals did not want black soldiers. Still, freedmen in Pittsburgh, Pennsylvania; Cleveland, Ohio; Boston, Massachusetts; and other cities in the North rallied to the cause. They wanted to wear Union blues and stand up for their country.

In the South, slaves fled their homes to seek refuge and freedom with Northern troops. Escaped slaves were considered "contrabands"—Southern "property" confiscated by the North. The Union used African American volunteers as laborers to build dikes and ditches. By 1863 the U.S. government officially recruited African Americans. More than 180,000 volunteered. They proudly wore Federal uniforms, fighting for the Union and for freedom.

Top: Two brothers wear their Union uniforms in this photo. *Bottom:* African American troops from the District of Columbia pose with their rifles at Fort Lincoln in Washington, D.C., in 1865.

These workers, shown in 1865, were employed by the Union army at a trimming shop in Washington, D.C., which made supplies for Northern troops.

MASS PRODUCTION

Outfitting an entire army requires money, effort, and time. The Civil War marked the first time factories mass-produced clothing. They whipped out stacks and stacks of uniforms to outfit Northern troops.

Factory-made clothes led to another first: standard sizes. The Civil War was the first time manufacturers agreed on standard sizing. Until the war, customers just looked around until they found items that fit. Standard sizing helped the military outfit troops more efficiently.

A new machine patented in 1862 made shoes faster by sewing the upper part of the shoe to the sole. That helped resupply the Union army with shoes and boots, essential gear for soldiers on long marches.

Most U.S. factories, making everything from shoes and clothes to tents and guns, were in the North. That gave the Union a major advantage. Factories churned out Federal uniforms, boots, and weapons. Northern factories couldn't get Southern-grown cotton

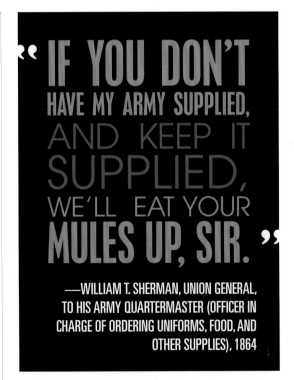

"**IF YOU DON'T** HAVE MY ARMY SUPPLIED, AND KEEP IT SUPPLIED, WE'LL EAT YOUR **MULES UP, SIR.**"

—WILLIAM T. SHERMAN, UNION GENERAL, TO HIS ARMY QUARTERMASTER (OFFICER IN CHARGE OF ORDERING UNIFORMS, FOOD, AND OTHER SUPPLIES), 1864

during the war, so they used wool for almost all clothing.

CONFEDERATE GRAY—
then Butternut

The North had factories, machines, railroads, and money. The South had cotton and tobacco and other agricultural goods. When Union ships blockaded (closed) Southern ports, the Confederacy couldn't sell its goods. The blockade also prevented the South from getting supplies—food, clothes, and weapons—from Europe. The lack of money and machines deeply hurt the Confederate effort.

The South had cotton but no way to manufacture it, so most Confederate uniforms were homemade. The Confederacy chose gray for its uniforms because gray dye was cheap. When the war began, a Confederate soldier was supposed to wear

- **A GRAY WOOL JACKET**
- *light blue trousers*
- **A BELT WITH A BRASS BUCKLE** (buckles were stamped CSA, or CS, for Confederate States of America)
- *a white cotton shirt*
- **SHOES**
- **A HAT** (usually a broad felt slouch hat but sometimes a kepi)

Most Confederate soldiers wore waist-length jackets, double breasted with two rows of gilt buttons. Gray Jackets became a nickname for Confederate soldiers. By 1863 the South had used all its gray dye, so military families made dyes from white walnut shells and rusty iron soaked in water. The homemade mixture turned uniforms a yellowy-tan, a color called butternut. Sometimes Confederate soldiers were called Butternuts.

This Confederate cavalry officer wears a gray uniform frock coat. As the war progressed and supplies dwindled, more CSA soldiers wore shorter jackets that required less fabric. He carries a slouch hat and a glove in his right hand.

Above: This hat shows the yellowy-tan color of Confederate uniforms. It belonged to Confederate general Thomas "Stonewall" Jackson.

Making Do

While Union troops were issued new clothes once a year, the South didn't have an easy way to make new clothes and gear. Confederate troops tried to make their own shoes from cowhide that hadn't been tanned. But the shoes quickly rotted. In 1862 Confederate president Jefferson Davis assigned two thousand soldiers to make shoes full-time.

Without factories to make supplies quickly, the South ran low on many items. Southerners improvised. When the Confederate cavalry couldn't find cows to make leather for their saddles and bridles, troops waded into Mississippi swamps to hunt alligators. The swamp search succeeded, and Southern horsemen ended up with high-class alligator leather goods.

When Confederate troops needed coats, civilians scrounged to help. People in Savannah, Georgia, donated their carpets to the cause. The used carpets were cut up and sewn into uniforms. The leftover rugs were turned into five hundred blankets to keep Confederate troops warm.

Throughout the war, Confederate troops wore more varied clothes and less standard uniforms than Northern soldiers did. Southern soldiers struggled just to have any kind of clothes and shoes. Some resorted to taking uniforms and shoes from dead Union soldiers after battles. They tried unsuccessfully to boil the blue dye out of the Union clothes. In 1864 the North warned Confederate soldiers to stop wearing Union blue. Any Southern soldier caught in blue would be killed.

> ❝ **YOU GOT ON SICH A NICE NEW UNIFORM,** YOU GOT SICH NICE **BOOTS ON. YOU RIDIN' SICH A NICE HOSS, AN'** YOU LOOK LIKE **YER BOWELS WAS** SO REGULAR. ❞
>
> —CONFEDERATE SOLDIER COMPLIMENTING A UNION SOLDIER, 1865

This photo of Confederate army private Thomas Taylor shows his uniform and supplies in fairly good shape. Many Confederate soldiers struggled to find clothing and basic supplies as the Civil War dragged on.

WOMEN'S CLOTHES
HELPED THE WAR EFFORT

Many women found creative ways to help their side's soldiers:

- Two Virginia women, Elizabeth Van Lew and Mary Elizabeth Bowser, helped the Union army using sewing skills and a little ingenuity. Bowser was a free African American. She'd once been Van Lew's slave. Van Lew got Bowser into Confederate president Jefferson Davis's house so she could spy. Then Bowser passed information to Van Lew, who wrote messages in code on dress patterns that were sent north.

- Other Virginia women gave their clothes to help the South after the North launched hot air balloons to observe Confederate troop positions. The South wanted to send up its own balloon but didn't have material. Virginia women donated hundreds of their best dresses to the project. They were sewn together into what General James Longstreet called the Last Silk Dress in the Confederacy. The dramatic balloon dress didn't last long, though. Union troops captured it the first time it flew.

- Some women spies used their bulky clothes to help smuggle secrets. Confederate spy Rose O'Neal Greenhow *(right)* was on her way to deliver money and documents to Jefferson Davis. Greenhow had sewn her secret stash, including gold coins, into her gown. When the boat she was in capsized, Greenhow drowned, weighed down by heavy clothes and coins.

NATIVE TROOPS

Many Native Americans fought in the Civil War. About twelve thousand American Indians joined the Confederate army, while another three thousand fought for the North. One Cherokee, Stand Watie *(right)*, became a Confederate general. Watie was the Civil War's highest-ranking Native American soldier.

Some Native American soldiers combined traditional American Indian clothes, jewelry, and headbands with standard military uniforms. "Their dress was chiefly Indian costume," one observer said. "[They wore] buckskin hunting shirts dyed almost every color, leggings, and moccasins of the same material, with little bells, rattles, ear-rings, and similar paraphernalia."

Members of Union general Ulysses S. Grant's staff pose in front of Grant's headquarters in Virginia. Lieutenant Colonel Ely S. Parker *(second from right)*, Grant's military secretary, was a member of the Seneca Nation, a Native American tribe of the northeastern United States.

OPPOSING OFFICERS,
OPPOSING STYLES

Ulysses S. Grant was the highest-ranking U.S. general since George Washington. But Grant didn't dress the part. The man who is still considered one of the greatest U.S. generals didn't like wearing a military uniform.

Long before the Civil War, people in his hometown had laughed at young Ulysses Grant in uniform. Back then, Grant was a short and thin cadet at the army's U.S. Military Academy at West Point, New York. Grant said that being mocked "gave me distaste for military uniform that I never recovered from."

During the Civil War, Grant, commander of all Union forces, preferred a simple sack coat uniform, the kind worn by low-ranking soldiers. At Appomattox, where the South surrendered in 1865, Grant wore muddy boots and a dirty shirt borrowed from a private.

On the other side, Confederate general Robert E. Lee arrived at Appomattox in his finest full-dress uniform, complete with sash and fancy sword. Lee told his aide that he expected to become Grant's prisoner and "thought I must make my best appearance." In victory and defeat, Lee always seemed to make his best appearance. During the Civil War, Lee often wore a civilian frock coat and didn't wear the full insignia of a general. Still, the Southerner always looked like a commander.

Lee and Grant had different attitudes toward their appearance. But both men proved their leadership during the grueling war—a war that proved that clothes do not make the man.

The two top generals in the Civil War, Confederate general Robert E. Lee *(top)* and Union general Ulysses S. Grant *(left)*, had vastly different styles. In these photos, Grant's boots aren't as shined as Lee's, and his uniform is more worn and rumpled. Lee always took care to look the part of a high-ranking general.

Chapter Five

DESIGNERS and INVENTIONS

In 1858 in Paris, France, an Englishman named Charles Frederick Worth opened the House of Worth, which would become the first haute couture (high fashion) business. Stylish dresses and other garments were designed and made there.

Worth is considered the first modern fashion designer. The House of Worth made clothes—and history. Until Charles Worth came on the fashion scene, designers didn't control style. Customers decided what they wanted, and dressmakers followed those instructions. Worth created a new kind of high fashion by creating clothes for specific customers instead of letting them dictate to him.

Worth was the first designer to

- **hire models**, called mannequins, to show his clothes to customers. Worth's models looked like his best customers. When a customer gained weight, Worth told his model to do the same. Customers saw dresses on models that looked just as they would look on them.
- **use special lights** to show his clothes. At his carefully designed House of Worth salon, he blocked all natural light in one room and lit it solely by gaslight. The soft and glittering lighting let women see how gowns would look at nighttime parties. Worth's mood lighting helped sell dresses.

Englishman Charles Frederick Worth changed the way women dressed in the United States and around the world in the 1860s. He started the world's first haute couture (high fashion) business with a salon in Paris, France.

- **offer an entire season's collection** of outfits instead of creating just a few items
- **put his name on all the clothes** he created. The simple yet classic pink and gold House of Worth labels stood for style.

Worth is credited with dethroning the crinoline. But he still needed to use lots of fabric to keep French silk makers happy and employed, so Worth wrapped lots of fabric at the back of a dress, leaving the front simple and straighter. In 1864 Worth unveiled a new look—the bustle.

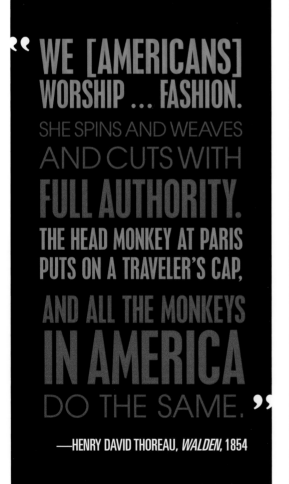

" **WE [AMERICANS] WORSHIP … FASHION.** SHE SPINS AND WEAVES AND CUTS WITH **FULL AUTHORITY.** THE HEAD MONKEY AT PARIS PUTS ON A TRAVELER'S CAP, AND ALL THE MONKEYS **IN AMERICA** DO THE SAME. "

—HENRY DAVID THOREAU, *WALDEN,* 1854

This ball gown by Charles Frederick Worth shows a bustle in the back. Bustles were the rage in American fashion in the late 1800s.

THE QUEENS OF FASHION

Decades before *People* magazine and *Project Runway*, people who cared about clothes looked to two women to set style: Queen Victoria of Britain and Empress Eugénie of France *(right)*.

Victoria wore only British-made clothing, which gave a great boost to her country's clothes makers and fabrics. Spanish-born Eugénie loved clothes and wanted the latest looks. Eugénie wore a crinoline decorated with pink-and-black bows and lace to meet Victoria in 1855. The British queen adopted the French-style crinoline, and soon crinoline cages were popular throughout Europe and the United States.

As she grew older, Victoria grew less interested in fashion. She didn't like spending time being fitted for new clothes. She ordered her dressmaker to sew several dresses in the same style but different fabrics.

In 1861 Victoria's interest in fashion plunged when her husband, Albert, died suddenly at the age of forty-two. The bereft queen dressed in black mourning clothes, no longer interested in style. Victoria wore only somber colors for the next forty years until her death in 1901.

A RAINBOW
OF NEW COLORS

Another fashion innovator never designed clothes, but his influence was still easy to spot. In 1856 English chemist William Henry Perkin invented a synthetic dye that made new colors. For the first time in history, people could wear clothes in colors not found in nature. Perkin's aniline dyes were cheaper than natural dyes and produced bolder, brighter colors. Mauve, a shade of violet purple, was everywhere. Soon other new synthetic colors popped up. They had outlandish names such as "nile-water" and "frightened mouse."

William Henry Perkin's synthetic dye invention introduced new and bold colors into world fashion in the 1860s.

Right: This silk dress from 1862 was dyed using William Henry Perkin's mauve dye. This was a popular color for fashion after Perkin's dye discovery.

Savile Row's
BESPOKE SUITS

While Perkin created new colors and Worth reshaped women's fashions, another Englishman found fame sewing men's suits. In the 1840s, Henry Poole became the first tailor to set up shop on Savile Row in London, England. Poole focused on personalized service and bespoke tailoring—which lets customers select precisely the details they want in the finished suit. French emperor Napoleon III, Great Britain's Prince of Wales, and author Charles Dickens all wore Poole's suits.

One of Poole's suit jackets made for the Prince of Wales caused a sensation across the Atlantic. The jacket was unusually short, and it was formal enough for evening wear. An American customer named James Potter asked Poole to make him a jacket just like it. When Potter returned to his home in Tuxedo Park, New York, his friends also wanted to own short jackets. Soon the jackets were all the rage among men. People began calling them tuxedos, for the New York town in which the style was first spotted. Henry Poole & Co. still makes and sells tuxedo jackets and other fine men's clothing. The shop is still located on London's Savile Row, a street known worldwide for custom clothing.

Henry Poole & Co. still resides on Savile Row in London, England. A modern version of one of their signature styles—the tuxedo—is shown in the window below. The tuxedo gets its name from Tuxedo Park, New York, home to James Potter, who was one of the first Americans to ask Poole to make him a jacket like the Prince of Wales wore.

SINGER'S *Revolutionary Machine*

In 1850 Isaac Merritt Singer changed the clothing world forever. Singer is credited with making the world's first practical sewing machine. Other inventors had tinkered with various sewing-machine models. But the groundbreaking shift happened when Singer saw a machine made by fellow American Elias Howe. Singer quickly improved on Howe's version. Once he had perfected his machine, he had it patented. In five years, Singer's company had stitched its way to being the world's biggest maker of sewing machines.

Machines can sew much faster than even the nimblest human. A skilled woman could sew thirty stitches a minute. In the same time, a machine could whip out seven thousand stitches. By using machines, people could produce a lot more clothing for less money. Clothes suddenly became easier to make—and much less expensive too.

This photograph shows an early model of the Singer sewing machine.

In the 1850s, Isaac Merritt Singer invented the first practical sewing machine that could be used at home.

A MACHINE IN EVERY HOME

At first, Singer sewing machines were used only in factories. But in 1856, Singer developed the world's first sewing machine for home use. That allowed women to make high-quality clothes at home more easily. Singer's bulky black machine changed women's lives. They didn't have to spend hours painstakingly sewing everything by hand.

In addition to inventing sewing machines, Singer was a super salesman. His company came up with the idea of installment purchases, which it called the hire-purchase plan. A customer could make a five-dollar down payment on a one-hundred-dollar machine and go home with it that day. Sales soared. Singer's company went from selling 2,564 machines in 1856 to 20,000 machines by 1861.

Singer's installment plan made his "A Machine in Every Home" motto seem possible. Sewing machines were the first home appliance. By 1863 Singer had stores in France, Brazil, and Germany, plus a factory in Scotland. Singer's business savvy made his company among the first multinational companies in the world.

Ebenezer Butterick's first dress patterns were made for his young son's clothes. Later, he sold them to the public so they could make their own clothes at home.

A PATTERN
FOR SEWING SUCCESS

Thanks to sewing machines, clothes quickly became more complicated. Designers dreamed up complex layers of frills and ruffles that would have been too time-consuming to sew by hand. Women who wanted to keep up with the latest look needed help re-creating those fussy fashions. That spurred a new industry—paper patterns.

Made of thin tissue paper, paper patterns showed people step-by-step instructions for making an item of clothing. It seemed as if everyone wanted to buy paper patterns to sew the latest fashions at home. Even Queen Victoria wanted patterns for her sons' clothes. She turned to the leader in patterns, an American named Ebenezer Butterick. Butterick was a bespoke tailor whose wife, Ellen, wished for a dress pattern for their little boy. In 1863 E. Butterick & Co. became the first company to sell patterns in multiple sizes.

At first, Butterick sold patterns only for men's and boy's clothes. But by 1866, the company added women's patterns. Then Butterick offered magazines featuring its patterns. It seemed every woman wanted to sew stylish clothes at home. And with sewing machines and patterns, she could.

A GREAT MAGAZINE
AND A FAMILIAR RHYME

Sarah Josepha Hale wasn't afraid to speak her mind. For forty years, Hale boldly edited one of America's most popular magazines, *Godey's Lady's Book*. This magazine bore the name of its founder, Louis A. Godey. But Hale, a widow with five children, transformed the magazine—and along with it, American culture.

Soon after she started working at the magazine in 1837, Hale began publishing works written by American authors and poets such as Nathaniel Hawthorne, Edgar Allan Poe, and Henry Wadsworth Longfellow. She also published three issues dedicated solely to women writers.

Godey's wasn't all words. Hale added color fashion plates—dainty, hand-drawn pictures of stylish clothes. She hired artists to re-create copies of fashions from European magazines. Hale—who dressed in black mourning clothes for decades after her husband's death—knew that fashion sold magazines. Under Hale, *Godey's* circulation rose from 25,000 readers in 1839 to 150,000 readers in 1860.

In 1877, after four decades as editor, Hale stepped down. She had molded a magazine, promoted great writers and ideas, and also found some time to publish dozens of her own books. Her most popular work, though, remains a rhyme she wrote before becoming editor. Chances are you even know a bit of Sarah Josepha Hale's work by heart. It starts out, "Mary had a little lamb."

This illustration is from the October 1864 edition of *Godey's Lady's Book*. The magazine showed popular fashions of the day.

The Cast Iron Palace department store was built in the early 1860s in New York City by Alexander Turney Stewart, an Irish immigrant.

Ready to Wear

Until the mid-1800s, almost all clothes were either made at home or by a tailor. Tailors made clothes specially fitted for each customer. But not everyone had time or money for tailor fittings. By mid-century, spinning mills churned out fabric faster, which made it easier to make clothes faster.

Soon U.S. factories were turning out ready-to-wear clothes. People could go to stores and buy clothes off the rack rather than going to a tailor and being fitted for clothes that took days or weeks to make.

Some tailors started offering ready-to-wear clothes. But by the 1860s, a new kind of store emerged to sell them. The Civil War era marked the birth of department stores, which offered floors full of clothes, furniture, rugs, housewares, and toys.

In 1862 Irish immigrant Alexander Turney Stewart opened the Cast Iron Palace, an eight-story department store that took up an entire New York City block. The new store offered nineteen departments—almost like individual shops—for everything from silks to glassware. Within a few years, New Yorkers had a "Ladies Mile" district of department stores along Broadway, including Lord & Taylor's, B. Altman's, and Macy's.

Not everyone was happy about the new department stores. The *New York World* complained about the stores and the newly wealthy people who shopped in them. "They set or follow the shoddy [cheap and vulgar] fashions," the *World* said. "[They] fondly imagine themselves à la mode de Paris [in the style of Paris], when they are only à la mode de shoddy [in the style of the cheap and vulgar]."

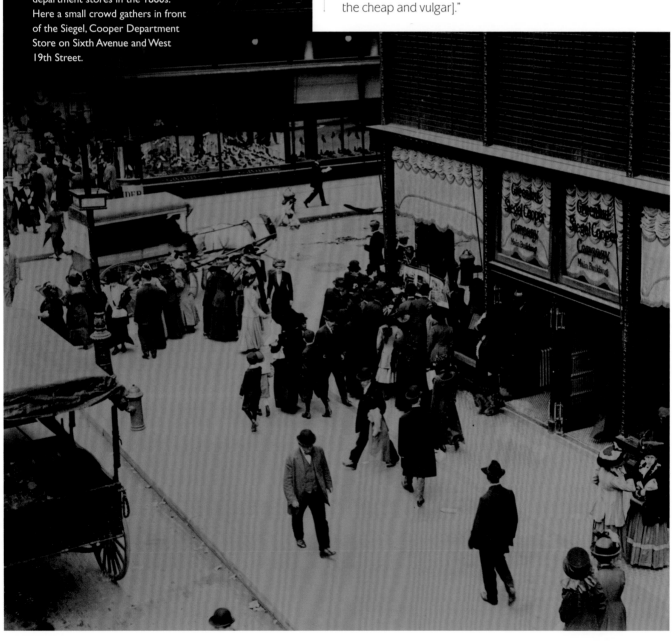

Ladies Mile shopping district in New York City featured many department stores in the 1860s. Here a small crowd gathers in front of the Siegel, Cooper Department Store on Sixth Avenue and West 19th Street.

FIRST LADY OF SHOPPING

First Lady Mary Todd Lincoln loved to shop. She shopped when she was bored, lonely, or sad. When her family moved into the White House in 1861, Mary went shopping to update the mansion's public and private spaces. She overspent her budget and tried to hide it from the president. He found out and got angry.

Mary's shopping habit got worse, especially after the Lincoln's eleven-year-old son Willie died of a fever in 1862. Supposedly, the First Lady bought four hundred pairs of gloves in just three months. She also purchased clothing that she never unwrapped.

After Lincoln's assassination in 1865, Mary left Washington, taking her sons and sixty-four trunks of belongings with her. Six months later, she tried to pay off her debts by selling a ballroomful of her dresses and belongings. But instead of buying the clothes, the public mocked her. The press even called the sale "Mrs. Lincoln's Second Hand Clothing Sale." Later on, Mary received a large sum of money when Lincoln's estate (his property and money) was settled. In 1875 Mary's only surviving son, Robert, had Mary committed to a sanatorium for the mentally ill, mostly because she spent too much money.

Shoddy or not, department stores helped create a new trend of mass consumption. Shopping became a hobby, and Americans soon had plenty of places to look and buy. Shoppers could also spend their time and money in smaller, specialized stores. One of the most popular jewelry shops from Civil War times is still around. Charles Lewis Tiffany opened his first fancy goods store in New York in 1837. By 1845 Tiffany & Company had published the first mail-order catalog in the United States. Lincoln bought a Tiffany seed pearl set of bracelets, a necklace, earrings, and a brooch for his wife, Mary, to wear to his first inauguration in 1861. He paid $530. These days, the matching pearl jewelry would cost $13,000. (The Library of Congress has Mary's pearls, so they're not for sale.)

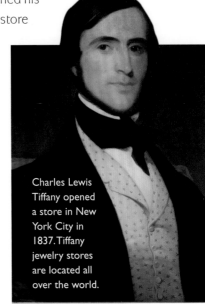

Charles Lewis Tiffany opened a store in New York City in 1837. Tiffany jewelry stores are located all over the world.

Mary Todd Lincoln poses in the Tiffany jewelry her husband, President Abraham Lincoln, bought for her. She wore it to her husband's first inaugural ball in 1861. This photo was taken by famous photographer Mathew Brady.

A female employee works at a garment factory in New York City in the early 1900s.

EPILOGUE

By the end of the Civil War, life for Americans had changed forever. People and events far from the battlefields helped steer the country in new directions. The tradition of homespun clothes was past. A new era of machine-made clothing had begun. Much of that clothing went to department stores, another of the era's innovations. These giant stores—palaces designed to encourage people to buy—rang in a new age of shopping and mass consumption.

Clothing in department stores was mostly made by girls and women. They worked twelve hours a day in wretched conditions in textile mills and factories. These mills and factories were sweatshops—workplaces that were crowded, hot, and often dangerous. Many women lugged their own sewing machines from home each day to use on the job in clothing factories. Young workers often earned less than three dollars a week. Orphans who worked in mills sometimes weren't paid anything at all.

BUY BY MAIL, *Buy in Store*

While laborers and millworkers struggled to get by, middle-class Americans were buying more. They browsed through catalogs from big retailers such as Sears, Roebuck and Co. and Montgomery Ward.

Around the country, store shelves bulged with loads of clothes and other goods. As the Victorian era ended, people clamored for more comfortable clothes. Jeans continued to be a fashion favorite. In 1886 Levi Strauss introduced his Two Horse Brand, the same logo on jeans sold in the twenty-first century. Another classic of the time was Gustav Jaeger's one-piece union suits, called long johns, made of wool and worn year-round by millions of men.

THE NEXT NEW THINGS

By the end of the 1800s, the craze for bicycles created demand for sportier clothes. Women wore bloomer pants to ride bikes. Hemlines rose above the ankle so women could ride and walk more easily. Bike-riding men and women needed better boots and smaller hats. Men started wearing visored caps, which resembled modern baseball caps. The Cincinnati Red Stockings baseball team scored a fashion home run when they first took the field in visored caps in 1869.

By the early 1900s, men were flocking to stores for the newest consumer item—a safety razor, which made it easier for men to shave at home. Men wore three-piece suits, with sack coats, vests, and trousers in matching colors. Traveling men who crisscrossed the country on trains needed another new fashion item—pajamas. The loose-fitting shirts and pants were more practical for businessmen spending nights on a sleeper train.

Around 1900 the ideal for American women was the Gibson Girl. Illustrator Charles Dana Gibson sketched countless images of this dream girl, with thin neck and waist and full chest and hips. The Gibson Girl wore a shirtwaist—a simple blouse tailored like a man's business shirt with high collar and a full skirt. It became the uniform for working women. The streamlined shirtwaist suited the modern era, when women first got office jobs where they used the latest technology, a typewriter.

Innovations in technology and machines, from early cars to modern planes, continued to transform how Americans dressed. From early twentieth-century automobile bonnets to twenty-first century technical fabric running shirts with iPod pockets, clothes are made to fit our lives.

Riding bicycles—and the adjustments in clothing that made it easier for women to ride them—became popular toward the end of the 1800s. These bike riders head into the woods in 1880.

TIMELINE

1837 Charles Lewis Tiffany opens Tiffany & Company, a fancy goods store in New York.

1845 Tiffany & Company publishes the first mail-order catalog in the United States.

1846 Henry Poole opens his Savile Row tailor shop in London, England.

1849 The gold rush begins in California and Nevada.

1851 I. M. Singer patents the first practical home sewing machine.
Amelia Bloomer writes about a new look—women's trousers.

1856 The cage crinoline debuts in Paris, France.
William Henry Perkin invents synthetic aniline dyes.

1858 Charles Frederick Worth opens the first haute couture house, with a salon in Paris.

1860 Henry Poole makes the first tuxedo.

1861 The Civil War begins.

1862 The Cast Iron Palace opens in New York, becoming the first true U.S. department store.

1863 Ebenezer Butterick sells the first patterns with multiple sizes.

1864 Charles Frederick Worth introduces the bustle.

1865 The Civil War ends.
John B. Stetson starts making Stetson hats.

1869 The Cincinnati Red Stockings team wears early versions of baseball caps.

bloomers: wide-cut pants for women. Bloomers were named for Amelia Bloomer, who was the most famous woman to wear them.

boater: a flat-topped straw hat worn by men and women

brogans: sturdy, ankle-high men's shoes

burnsides: an early name for sideburns. Burnsides were named for Union general Ambrose Burnside. They were also known as mutton chops.

bustle: a type of women's dress with a large pad of fabric at the back

Butternuts: a nickname for Confederate soldiers, whose uniforms were sometimes dyed yellowish tan

cameo: a popular kind of women's jewelry featuring a carved silhouette of a person

chignon: a classic hairstyle for women featuring a bun of hair at the nape of the neck

Confederate gray: the gray uniform color worn by Southern soldiers in the Civil War

corset: a women's fitted undergarment worn to shape the hips, the waist, and the bust

cravat: a men's tie made with a wide piece of silk or other fabric

derby: a formal hat for men

drawers: men's underwear that extended from the waist to the ankle

frock coat: a common knee-length men's jacket

gaiters: a pant and boot covering for men, made of leather or cloth. Gaiters protected a man's pants and boots.

kepi: a squashed-looking cap worn by most Union and some Confederate soldiers. It was also called a forage cap.

paisley: a popular type of teardrop-shaped pattern used for shawls and other items. It was named for Paisley, Scotland, where it was first woven.

pantalets: long, loose underwear worn under women's and girls' skirts

pantaloons: men's long pants

spats: a cloth leg covering used to protect men's shoes and pants. Spats was short for splatterdashes.

Stetson: a cowboy hat named for Philadelphia hatmaker John Batterson Stetson

tailcoat: a fashionable formal men's coat with knee-length tails in back. Tailcoats were also known as swallowtails or claw hammers.

top hat: a traditional hat for men. Top hats were also called stovepipe hats, chimney pots, or opera hats.

tuxedo: a men's formal suit jacket made popular in Tuxedo, New York

Union blue: a dark blue uniform color worn by Northern soldiers in the Civil War

SOURCE NOTES

5   *New York Times*, "New-Jersey.; A Young Lady Dragged Two Miles by Runaway Horses," June 17, 1865, 2011. http://www.nytimes .com/1865/06/17/news/new-jersey-a-young-lady-dragged-two-miles-by-runaway-horses.html?scp=1&sq=Young+Lady+Dragg ed+Two+Miles+by+Runaway+Horses&st=p (March 30, 2011).

6   *Harper's New Monthly Magazine*, Editor's Drawer, "A Modern Belle," April 1853, available online at http://www1.assumption .edu/WHW/ModernBelle.html (March 30, 2011).

8   *Harper's New Monthly Magazine*, "Summer Fashions," July 1851, available online at http://www.gutenberg.org/ files/25093/25093-h/25093-h .htm#Editors_Drawer (March 30, 2011).

17 Allan Pinkerton, *Thirty Years a Detective* (New York: 1599 Books, 2007), 36.

25 Grace Bedell, letter to Abraham Lincoln, 1860, Burton Historical Collection, Detroit Public Library, Detroit, available online at http://www.detroitpubliclibrary.org/ LincolnCollection/lincoln_collection/ bh005001.html (March 30, 2011).

25 Ibid.

25 Ibid.

26 Frederick Douglass, *Narrative of the Life of Frederick Douglass, an American Slave* (Charleston, SC: BiblioLife, 2008), 22.

27 Ibid. 33.

28 Booker T. Washington, *Up from Slavery: An Autobiography*, available online at http:// xroads.virginia.edu/~HYPER/WASHINGTON/ ch01.html (March 23, 2011).

28 Clayton Holbert, interviewed by Leta Gray, American Guides, May 17, 1937, in *The American Slave*, supp. series 2, vol. 1 (Westport CT: Grenwood Press, 1972), 285, available online at http://xroads.virginia .edu/~hyper/wpa/holbert1.html (March 23, 2011).

28 Booker T. Washington, *Up from Slavery*.

29 Tempe Herndon Durham, interviewed by Travis Jordan, *The American Slave: North Carolina Narratives* 14, no.1, 286, available online at http://xroads.virginia.edu/~hyper/ wpa/durham1.html (March 23, 2011).

38 Marc McCutcheon, *Everyday Life in the 1800s: A Guide for Writers, Students and Historians* (Cincinnati: Writer's Digest Books, 2001), 225.

40 Catherine Clinton, *Scholastic Encyclopedia of the Civil War* (New York: Scholastic, 1999), 73.

41 Kate Havelin, *Ulysses S. Grant* (Minneapolis: Twenty-First Century Books, 2004), 15.

41 Douglas Freeman, *R.E. Lee: A Biography*, (New York: Charles Scribner's & Son, 1934), available online at http://penelope.uchicago .edu/Thayer/E/Gazetteer/People/Robert_E_ Lee/FREREL/home.html (March 23, 2011).

43 Henry David Thoreau, *Walden; or Life in the Woods*, n.d., available online at http://xroads .virginia.edu/~HYPER/WALDEN/walden.html (March 23, 2011).

51 Carl Sandburg, *Abraham Lincoln: The Prairie Years and the War Years*, Google Books online edition, 382, http://books.google .com/books?id=_nL5xCYLFs0C&printsec=fro ntcover&dq=Abraham+Lincoln&hl=en&ei=Li-TTdSeA4Wjtgf-ub1i&sa=X&oi=book_result&ct =result&resnum=5&ved=0CEsQ6AEwBA#v= onepage&q&f=false (March 30, 2011).

SELECTED BIBLIOGRAPHY

Biel, Timothy Levi. *Life in the North during the Civil War*. San Diego: Lucent Books, 1997.

Blum, Stella, ed. *Fashions and Costumes from Godey's Lady's Book*. Mineola, NY: Dover Publications, 1985.

Boucher, Francois. *20,000 Years of Fashion: The History of Costume and Personal Adornment*. New York: Harry N. Abrams, 1987.

Clinton, Catherine. *Scholastic Encyclopedia of the Civil War*. New York: Scholastic, 1999.

Corrick, James A. *The Civil War: Life among the Soldiers and Cavalry*. San Diego: Lucent Books, 2000.

Cosgrave, Bronwyn. *The Complete History of Costume and Fashion from Ancient Egypt to the Present Day*. New York: Facts on File, 2000.

Donald, David Herbert. *Lincoln at Home: Two Glimpses of Abraham Lincoln's Family Life*. New York: Simon & Schuster, 1999.

Douglass, Frederick. *Narrative of the Life of Frederick Douglass, an American Slave*. Charleston, SC: BiblioLife, 2008.

Enss, Chris. *How the West Was Worn: Bustles and Buckskins on the Wild Frontier*. Guilford, CT: Pequot Globe Press, 2006.

Fleming, Candace. *The Lincolns: A Scrapbook Look at Abraham and Mary*. New York: Schwartz & Wade Books, 2008.

McCutcheon, Marc. *Everyday Life in the 1800s: A Guide for Writers, Students and Historians*. Cincinnati: Writer's Digest Books, 2001.

Picken, Mary Brooks. *A Dictionary of Costume and Fashion: Historic and Modern*. New York: Dover Publications, 1985.

Reger, James. P. *Life in the South during the Civil War*. San Diego: Lucent Books, 1997.

Schnurnberger, Lynn. *Let There Be Clothes: 40,000 Years of Fashion*. New York: Workman Publishing, 1991.

Taylor, Susie King. *A Black Woman's Civil War Memoirs: Reminiscences of My Life*. Princeton, NJ: Markus Wiener Publishers, 1997.

Washington, Booker T. *Up From Slavery: An Autobiography*. Available online at http://xroads.virginia.edu/~HYPER/WASHINGTON/ch01.html (March 23, 2011).

White, Shane, and Graham White. "Slave Clothing and African-American Culture in the Eighteenth and Nineteenth Centuries," *Past & Present*, August 1, 1995.

Williams, David. *A People's History of the Civil War: Struggles for the Meaning of Freedom*. New York: New York Press, 2005.

FURTHER READING AND WEBSITES

BOOKS

Boyle, David. *Coming to America: African Americans*. Hauppauge, NY: Barrons Educational Series (The Ivy Press Limited), 2003.

Damon, Duane. *Growing Up in the Civil War 1861–1865*. Minneapolis: Lerner Publications Company, 2003.

Day, Nancy. *Your Travel Guide to Civil War America*. Minneapolis: Twenty-First Century Books, 2001.

Draper, Allison Stark. *What People Wore during the Civil War*. New York: PowerKids Press, 2001.

Fleming, Candace. *The Lincolns: A Scrapbook Look at Abraham and Mary*. New York: Schwartz & Wade Books, 2008.

Havelin, Kate. *Ulysses S. Grant*. Minneapolis: Twenty-First Century Books, 2004.

Jess, Tyehimba. *African American Pride: Celebrating Our Achievements, Contributions and Enduring Legacy*. New York: Citadel Press, 2003.

Knauer, Kelly, ed. *Time: America; An Illustrated Early History 1776–1900*. New York: Time, 2007.

Miller, Brandon Marie. *Dressed for the Occasion: What Americans Wore 1620–1970*. Minneapolis: Twenty-First Century Books, 1999.

Sills, Leslie. *From Rags to Riches: A History of Girls' Clothing in America*. New York: Holiday House, 2005.

Swain, Ruth Freeman. *Underwear: What We Wear Under There*. New York: Holiday House, 2008.

WEBSITES

The Beard Community Bulletin Board
http://beardcommunity.com/
Images, photographs, and information about all kinds of beards are available at this site.

Corsets and Crinolines
http://www.corsetsandcrinolines.com
This site contains a visual timeline of the history of clothes.

The Costume Gallery
http://www.costumegallery.com/hairstyles
This site contains a collection of historical hairstyles.

Fanny & Vera
http://www.shasta.com/suesgoodco/newcivilians/womenswear/fashion.htm
This site provides a basic overview of women's clothing during the Civil War, with attention to making clothes for Civil War reenactments.

Frances Young Tang Teaching Museum and Art Gallery at Skidmore College
http://tang.skidmore.edu
The museum exhibits include "Hair: Untangling a Social History."

Kent State University Museum
http://dept.kent.edu
The museum exhibits include "Wrapped in Splendor: The Art of the Paisley Shawl" and "The Right Chemistry: Colors in Fashion, 1704–1918."

Library of Congress
http://loc.gov
The Library of Congress has a good collection of Civil War photographs. You can search the site with keywords such as *women*, *women's fashion*, *Civil War photography*, *soldiers' uniforms*, and other related terms.

Memorial Hall Museum Online, American Centuries, View from New England
http:www.memorialhall.mass.edu/activities/dressup/civil_war_soldier.html
This kid-friendly site includes an online collection, interactive activities, and primary sources on Civil War soldiers.

National Women's History Museum
http://nwhm.org
This site offers great biographies and online exhibits about American women's history.

Victoriana magazine
http://www.victorianamagazine.com
This site contains a section on Victorian fashions.

The Victorian Web
http://www.victorianweb.org
This academic site includes articles and essays about all things Victorian including fashions of the era.

Visit-Gettysburg.com
http://visit-Gettysburg.com/civil-war-clothes.html
This site offers a wealth of information about soldiers' uniforms, nurses' clothes, women's hairstyles and clothing, as well as material related to the Civil War itself.

Women's History Workshop
http://www1.assumption.edu/WHW
This website is the collaborative effort of Massachusetts teachers and features primary source materials about U.S. women's history, including during the Civil War era.

Women Writers
http://www.womenwriters.net
This e-zine contains a good article about Sarah Josepha Hale.

INDEX

ABOUT THE AUTHOR

Kate Havelin has written more than a dozen books for young people, including biographies of Queen Elizabeth I, Ulysses Grant, and Che Guevara. The Amelia Bloomer Project included her *Victoria Woodhull: Fearless Feminist* in its recommended list of books. Havelin has also written two trail guidebooks for adults, *Minnesota Running Trails: Dirt, Gravel, Rocks and Roots* and *Best Hikes of the Twin Cities*, both of which received awards from the Midwest Book Awards. When she's not writing, she likes to read, run, hike, kayak, ski, or snowshoe. Havelin lives in Saint Paul, Minnesota, with her husband and two teenage sons. You can visit her website, www.katehavelin.com.

PHOTO ACKNOWLEDGMENTS

The images in this book are used with the permission of: © Jameswimsel/Dreamstime.com, pp. 1, 56; The Granger Collection, New York, pp. 3, 8, 30, 45 (right), 48, 50; © Charles Clifford/Archive Farms/Hulton Archive/Getty Images, p. 4; © Bettmann/CORBIS, pp. 5, 6, 51, 55; Ohio Historical Society, p. 7; Virginia Historical Society, Richmond, Virginia (colorization), pp. 9, 14; © Cheltenham Art Gallery & Museums, Gloucestershire, UK/The Bridgeman Art Library, p. 10; © National Portrait Gallery, Smithsonian Institution/Art Resource, NY, p. 11; © Otto Herschan/Hulton Archive/Getty Images, p. 12; © G. H. Martyn/Otto Herschan/Hulton Archive/Getty Images, p. 13; © CORBIS, pp. 15 (top), 16, 36; Wisconsin Historical Society, WHi-30250 (alteration), p. 15 (bottom); © Mary Evans/Grosvenor Prints/The Image Works, p. 17; © Sean Sexton/Hulton Archive/Getty Images, p. 18; © Fotosearch/Archive Photos/Getty Images, p. 19 (top); © ullstein bild/The Image Works, p. 19 (bottom); © Hulton Deutsch Collection/CORBIS, p. 20 (left); The Art Archive/Bill Manns, p. 20 (right); © Hulton Archive/Getty Images, pp. 21 (top), 31, 42, 44, 47 (right); © Frederic Lewis/Archive Photos/ Getty Images, p. 21 (bottom left); Library of Congress, pp. 21 (bottom right, LC-DIG-cwpb-01142), 24 (left, LC-DIG-cwpb-06941), 24 (top right, LC-DIG-cwpb-05368), 24 (bottom right, LC-DIG-cwpb-04402), 25 (top, LC-USZ62-69580), 25 (bottom, LC-DIG-ppmsca-19301), 27 (LC-DIG-ppmsca-11182), 29 (LC-B8171-152-A), 32 (LC-USZC2-2991), 33 (top, LC-DIG-cwpbh-00520), 33 (bottom, LC-DIG-ppmsca-09867), 34 (left, LC-DIG-ppmsca-27237), 34 (right, LC-DIG-ppmsca-27531), 35 (top, LC-DIG-ppmsca-13484), 40 (bottom, LC-DIG-cwpb-02956), 47 (left, LC-DIG-hec-28455), 53 (LC-DIG-cwpbh-01027); © Civil War Archive/The Bridgeman Art Library, pp. 22, 37 (left); © Picture History, p. 23 (left); © Buyenlarge/Archive Photos/Getty Images, pp. 23 (right), 35 (bottom); The Art Archive/Culver Pictures, p. 26; © Dorling Kindersley/Getty Images, p. 28 (top); © MPI/Archive Photos/Getty Images, p. 28 (bottom); © Tria Giovan/CORBIS, p. 37 (right); © Peter Newark Military Pictures/The Bridgeman Art Library, pp. 38, 39; © Medford Historical Society Collection/ CORBIS, p. 40 (top); National Archives, pp. 41 (top, 111-B-1564), 41 (bottom, 111-B-36); Worth, Charles Frederick (1858-1956), Dress (Ball Gown), ca. 1872, silk, length at CB (a,b,c): 55 in. (139.8 cm), length (c): 23 in. (58.4 cm), Gift of Mrs. Philip K. Rhinelander, 1946 (46.25.1a-d), Image copyright © The Metropolitan Museum of Art/Art Resource, NY, p. 43; © SSPL/Science Museum/Art Resource, NY, p. 45 (left); © Tim Graham/Tim Graham Photo Library/Getty Images, p. 46; © Transcendental Graphics/Archive Photos/Getty Images, p. 49; © Collection of the New-York Historical Society, USA/The Bridgeman Art Library, p. 52; © Brown Brothers, p. 54.
Front cover: Library of Congress (LC-DIG-cwpbh-03059). Back cover: Library of Congress (LC-USZ62-129680).

Main body text provided by Mixage ITC Book 10/15
Typeface provided by International Typeface Corp